The
AMERICAN
FLAG

Thank you for purchasing an Applewood Book.
Applewood reprints America's lively classics—
books from the past that are still
of interest to modern readers.
For a free copy of our current catalog, write to:
Applewood Books, Box 27, Carlisle, MA 01741.

ISBN 978-1-55709-071-3

© 2013 Applewood Books Inc.

10 9 8 7 6

MANUFACTURED IN
THE UNITED STATES OF AMERICA
WITH AMERICAN-MADE MATERIALS

The

AMERICAN FLAG

A Handbook
of History & Etiquette

APPLEWOOD BOOKS

Carlisle, Massachusetts

In the late nineteenth century, many states adopted laws to defend the sacred character of the flag by prohibiting its use in commerce. After World War I, in 1923, a National Flag Conference held in Washington, D.C., adopted a set of provisions recognizing that the flag "represents a living country and is itself considered a living thing." On June 22, 1942, President Franklin D. Roosevelt approved a federal resolution that included many of the National Flag Conference's provisions codifying existing customs and rules governing the display and use of the flag of the United States by civilians. It was amended in December 1942. The Flag Code was reconfirmed during the U.S. Bicentennial in 1976 and its provisions were recodified in 1998 as part of Title 4. The Flag Code provides no penalties for noncompliance; rather it is a guide for civilians and civilian groups on how to display and show respect to the flag.

THE
FLAG CODE

★ ★ ★

Title 4, Chapter 1 of the United States Code details the laws relating to the flag of the United States of America.

1. The design of the flag

The flag of the United States shall be thirteen horizontal stripes, alternate red and white; and the union of the flag shall be forty-eight stars, white in a blue field.

2. A new star for each new state

On the admission of a new State into the Union one star shall be added to the union of the flag; and such addition shall take effect on the fourth day of July then next succeeding such admission.

3. Use of the flag or the Stars and Stripes in commerce within Washington, D.C.

Any person who, within the District of Columbia, in any manner, for exhibition or display, shall place or cause to be placed any word, figure, mark, picture, design, drawing, or any advertisement of any nature upon any flag, standard, colors, or ensign of the United States of America;

or shall expose or cause to be exposed to public view any such flag, standard, colors, or ensign upon which shall have been printed, painted, or otherwise placed, or to which shall be attached, appended, affixed, or annexed any word, figure, mark, picture, design, or drawing, or any advertisement of any nature; or who, within the District of Columbia, shall manufacture, sell, expose for sale, or to public view, or give away or have in possession for sale, or to be given away or for use for any purpose, any article or substance being an article of merchandise, or a receptacle for merchandise or article or thing for carrying or transporting merchandise, upon which shall have been printed, painted, attached, or otherwise placed a representation of any such flag, standard, colors, or ensign, to advertise, call attention to, decorate, mark, or distinguish the article or substance on which so placed shall be deemed guilty of a misdemeanor and shall be punished by a fine not exceeding $100 or by imprisonment for not more than thirty days, or both, in the discretion of the court. The words "flag, standard, colors, or ensign", as used herein, shall include any flag, standard, colors, ensign, or any picture or representation of either, or of any part or parts of either, made of any substance or represented on any substance, of any size evidently purporting to be either of said flag, standard, colors, or ensign of the United States of America or a picture or a representation of either, upon which shall be shown the colors, the stars and the stripes, in any number of either thereof, or of any part or parts of either, by which the average person seeing the same without deliberation may believe the same to represent the flag, colors, standard, or ensign of the United States of America.

4. The Pledge of Allegiance and how to act

The Pledge of Allegiance to the Flag: "I pledge allegiance to the Flag of the United States of America, and to the Republic for which it stands, one Nation under God, indivisible, with liberty and justice for all.", should be rendered by standing at attention facing the flag with the right hand over the heart. When not in uniform men should remove any non-religious headdress with their right hand and hold it at the left shoulder, the hand being over the heart. Persons in uniform should remain silent, face the flag, and render the military salute.

5. Display and use of flag by civilians; codification of rules and customs; definition

The following codification of existing rules and customs pertaining to the display and use of the flag of the United States of America shall be, and it is hereby, established for the use of such civilians or civilian groups or organizations as may not be required to conform with regulations promulgated by one or more executive departments of the Government of the United States. The flag of the United States for the purpose of this chapter shall be defined according to Title 4, United States Code, Chapter 1, Section 1 and Section 2 and Executive Order 10834 issued pursuant thereto.

6. Time and occasions for display

Display the flag from sunrise to sunset, but if properly illuminated it may be displayed day and night.

(a) It is the universal custom to display the flag only from sunrise to sunset on buildings and on stationary flagstaffs in the open. However, when a patriotic effect is desired, the flag may be displayed twenty-four hours a day if properly illuminated during the hours of darkness.

(b) The flag should be hoisted briskly and lowered ceremoniously.

(c) The flag should not be displayed on days when the weather is inclement, except when an all-weather flag is displayed.

(d) The flag should be displayed on all days, especially on New Year's Day, January 1; Inauguration Day, January 20; Martin Luther King Jr.'s Birthday, third Monday in January; Lincoln's Birthday, February 12; Washington's Birthday, third Monday in February; Easter Sunday (variable); Mother's Day, second Sunday in May; Armed Forces Day, third Saturday in May; Memorial Day (half-staff until noon), the last Monday in May; Flag Day, June 14; Father's Day, third Sunday in June; Independence Day, July 4; Labor Day, first Monday in September; Constitution Day, September 17; Columbus Day, second Monday in October; Navy Day, October 27; Veterans Day, November 11; Thanksgiving Day, fourth Thursday in November; Christmas Day, December 25; and such other days as may be proclaimed by the President of the United States; the birthdays of States (date of admission); and on State holidays.

Display the flag especially on these holidays.

(e) The flag should be displayed daily on or near the main administration building of every public institution.

(f) The flag should be displayed in or near every polling place on election days.

(g) The flag should be displayed during school days in or near every schoolhouse.

7. Position and manner of display

The flag, when carried in a procession with another flag or flags, should be either on the marching right; that is, the flag's own right, or, if there is a line of other flags, in front of the center of that line.

(a) The flag should not be displayed on a float in a parade except from a staff, or as provided in subsection (i) of this section.

(b) The flag should not be draped over the hood, top, sides, or back of a vehicle or of a railroad train or a boat. When the flag is displayed on a motorcar, the staff shall be fixed firmly to the chassis or clamped to the right fender.

No other flag should be placed above.

(c) No other flag or pennant should be placed above or, if on the same level, to the right of the flag of the United States of America, except during church services conducted by naval chaplains at sea, when the church pennant may be flown above the flag during church services for the personnel of the Navy. No person shall display the flag of the United Nations or any other national or international flag equal, above, or in a position of superior prominence or honor to, or in place of, the flag of the United States at any place within the United States or any Territory or possession thereof: Provided, that nothing in this section shall make unlawful the continuance of the practice heretofore followed of displaying the flag of the United Nations in a position of superior prominence or honor, and other national flags in positions of equal prominence or honor, with that of the flag of the United States at the headquarters of the United Nations.

(d) The flag of the United States of America, when it is displayed with another flag against a wall from crossed staffs, should be on the right, the flag's own right, and its staff should be in front of the staff of the other flag.

(e) The flag of the United States of America should be at the center and at the highest point of the group when a number of flags of States or localities or pennants of societies are grouped and displayed from staffs.

(f) When flags of States, cities, or localities, or pennants of societies are flown on the same halyard with the flag of the United States, the latter should always be at the peak. When the flags are flown from adjacent staffs, the flag of the United States should be hoisted first and lowered last. No such flag or pennant may be placed above the flag of the United States or to the United States flag's right.

(g) When flags of two or more nations are displayed, they are to be flown from separate staffs of the same height. The flags should be of approximately equal size. International usage forbids the display of the flag of one nation above that of another nation in time of peace.

(h) When the flag of the United States is displayed from a staff projecting horizontally or at an angle from the window sill, balcony, or front of a building, the union of the flag should be placed at the peak of the staff unless the flag is at half-staff. When the flag is suspended over a sidewalk from a rope extending from a house to a pole at the edge of the sidewalk, the flag should be hoisted out, union first, from the building.

(i) When displayed either horizontally or vertically against a wall, the union should be uppermost and to the flag's own right, that is, to the observer's left. When displayed in a window, the flag should be displayed in the same way, with the union or blue field to the left of the observer in the street.

(j) When the flag is displayed over the middle of the street, it should be suspended vertically with the union to the north in an east and west street or to the east in a north and south street.

(k) When used on a speaker's platform, the flag, if displayed flat, should be displayed above and behind the speaker. When displayed from a staff in a church or public auditorium, the flag of the United States of America should hold the position of superior prominence, in advance of the audience, and in the position of honor at the clergyman's or speaker's right as he faces the audience. Any other flag so displayed should be placed on the left of the clergyman or speaker or to the right of the audience.

(l) The flag should form a distinctive feature of the ceremony of unveiling a statue or monument, but it should never be used as the covering for the statue or monument.

(m) The flag, when flown at half-staff, should be first hoisted to the peak for an instant and then lowered to the half-staff position. The flag should be again raised to the peak before it is lowered for the day. On Memorial Day the flag should be displayed at half-staff until noon only, then raised to the top of the staff. By order of the President, the flag shall be flown at half-staff upon the death of principal figures of the United States Government and the Governor of a State, territory, or possession, as a mark of respect to their memory. In the event of the death of other officials or foreign dignitaries, the flag is to be displayed at half-staff according to Presidential instructions or orders, or in accordance with recognized customs or practices not inconsistent with law. In the event of the death of a present or former official of the government of any State, territory, or possession of the United States, or the death of a member of the Armed Forces from any State, territory, or possession who dies while serving on active duty, the Governor of that State, territory, or possession may proclaim that the National flag shall be flown at half-staff, and the same authority is provided

On Memorial Day, the flag should be half-staff until noon only.

to the Mayor of the District of Columbia with respect to present or former officials of the District of Columbia and members of the Armed Forces from the District of Columbia. The flag shall be flown at half-staff thirty days from the death of the President or a former President; ten days from the day of death of the Vice President, the Chief Justice or a retired Chief Justice of the United States, or the Speaker of the House of Representatives; from the day of death until interment of an Associate Justice of the Supreme Court, a Secretary of an executive or military department, a former Vice President, or the Governor of a State, territory, or possession; and on the day of death and the following day for a Member of Congress. The flag shall be flown at half-staff on Peace Officers Memorial Day, unless that day is also Armed Forces Day. As used in this subsection —

The flag should be flown at half-staff for thirty days after the death of a president.

(1) the term "half-staff" means the position of the flag when it is one-half the distance between the top and bottom of the staff;

(2) the term "executive or military department" means any agency listed under sections 101 and 102[1] of Title 5, United States Code; and

[1] See list on page 20.

(3) the term "Member of Congress" means a Senator, a Representative, a Delegate, or the Resident Commissioner from Puerto Rico.

A flag covering a casket should have the union at the head and over the left shoulder.

(n) When the flag is used to cover a casket, it should be so placed that the union is at the head and over the left shoulder. The flag should not be lowered into the grave or allowed to touch the ground.

(o) When the flag is suspended across a corridor or lobby in a building with only one main entrance, it should be suspended vertically with the union of the flag to the observer's left upon entering. If the building has more than one main entrance, the flag should be suspended vertically near the center of the corridor or lobby with the union to the north when entrances are to the east and west, or to the east when entrances are to the north and south. If there are entrances in more than two directions, the union should be to the east.

8. Respect for flag

No disrespect should be shown to the flag of the United States of America; the flag should not be dipped to any person or thing. Regimental colors, State flags, and organization or institutional flags are to be dipped as a mark of honor.

(a) The flag should never be displayed with the union down, except as a signal of dire distress in instances of extreme danger to life or property.

No disrespect should be shown the flag.

(b) The flag should never touch anything beneath it, such as the ground, the floor, water, or merchandise.

(c) The flag should never be carried flat or horizontally, but always aloft and free.

(d) The flag should never be used as wearing apparel, bedding, or drapery. It should never be festooned, drawn back, nor up, in folds, but always allowed to fall free. Bunting of blue, white, and red, always arranged with the blue above, the white in the middle, and the red below, should be used for covering a speaker's desk, draping the front of the platform, and for decoration in general.

(e) The flag should never be fastened, displayed, used, or stored in such a manner as to permit it to be easily torn, soiled, or damaged in any way.

(f) The flag should never be used as a covering for a ceiling.

(g) The flag should never have placed upon it, nor on any part of it, nor attached to it any mark, insignia, letter, word, figure, design, picture, or drawing of any nature.

(h) The flag should never be used as a receptacle for receiving, holding, carrying, or delivering anything.

Do not use the flag in advertising.

(i) The flag should never be used for advertising purposes in any manner whatsoever. It should not be embroidered on such articles as cushions or handkerchiefs and the like, printed or otherwise impressed on paper napkins or boxes or anything that is designed for temporary use and discard. Advertising signs should not be fastened to a staff or halyard from which the flag is flown.

(j) No part of the flag should ever be used as a costume or athletic uniform. However, a flag patch may be affixed to the uniform of military personnel, firemen, policemen, and members of patriotic organizations. The flag represents a living country and is itself considered a living thing. Therefore, the lapel flag pin being a replica, should be worn on the left lapel near the heart.

(k) The flag, when it is in such condition that it is no longer a fitting emblem for display, should be destroyed in a dignified way, preferably by burning.

Destroy a flag that is no longer a fitting emblem in a dignified way.

9. Conduct during hoisting, lowering, or passing of flag

During the ceremony of hoisting or lowering the flag or when the flag is passing in a parade or in review, all persons present in uniform should render the military salute. Members of the Armed Forces and veterans who are present but not in uniform may render the military salute. All other persons present should face the flag and stand at attention with their right hand over the heart, or if applicable, remove their headdress with their right hand and hold it at the left shoulder, the hand being over the heart. Citizens of other countries present should stand at attention. All such conduct toward the flag in a moving column should be rendered at the moment the flag passes.

10. Modification of rules and customs by President

Any rule or custom pertaining to the display of the flag of the United States of America, set forth herein, may be altered,

A president may modify any rule or custom.

modified, or repealed, or additional rules with respect thereto may be prescribed, by the Commander in Chief of the Armed Forces of the United States, whenever he deems it to be appropriate or desirable; and any such alteration or additional rule shall be set forth in a proclamation.

Title 5, Sections 101 and 102 of the United States Code detail which agencies shall have the flag flown half-staff from the day of death until interment.

Section 101

The Executive departments are:
- The Department of State.
- The Department of the Treasury.
- The Department of Defense.
- The Department of Justice.
- The Department of the Interior.
- The Department of Agriculture.
- The Department of Commerce.
- The Department of Labor.
- The Department of Health and Human Services.
- The Department of Housing and Urban Development.
- The Department of Transportation.
- The Department of Energy.
- The Department of Education.

- The Department of Veterans Affairs.
- The Department of Homeland Security.

Section 102

The military departments are:
- The Department of the Army.
- The Department of the Navy.
- The Department of the Air Force.

THE PLEDGE
OF ALLEGIANCE

★ ★ ★

The Pledge of Allegiance[2] received official recognition by Congress in an Act approved on June 22, 1942. However, the pledge was first written in 1892 by Francis Bellamy, an employee at *Youth's Companion* magazine and was first published on September 8, 1892, in the magazine, to celebrate the 400th anniversary of Columbus's arrival in America.

In its original version, the pledge read "my flag" instead of "the flag of the United States." The change in the wording was adopted by the National Flag Conference in 1923. The rationale for the change was that it prevented ambiguity among foreign-born children and adults who might have the flag of their native land in mind when reciting the pledge.

The phrase "under God" was added to the pledge by a congressional Act approved on June 14, 1954. At that time, President Eisenhower said: "In this way we are reaffirming the transcendence of religious faith in America's heritage and future; in this way we shall constantly strengthen those spiritual weapons which forever will be our country's most powerful resource in peace and war."

[2] See page 7.

22

FLAG PRESENTATION AND CARE

★ ★ ★

FLAG PRESENTATION

Presentation of the flag during a ceremony should be preceded by a brief talk emphasizing the importance of the occasion. Following the presentation all present should salute the flag, recite the Pledge of Allegiance, and sing the national anthem.

Precede the presentation of the flag with a brief talk emphasizing the importance of the occasion.

FOLDING THE FLAG

1. Two persons, facing each other, hold the flag waist high and horizontally between them.

2. The lower striped section is folded, lengthwise, over the blue field. Hold bottom to top and edges together securely.

3. Fold the flag again, lengthwise, folded edge to open edge.

4. A triangular fold is started along the length of the flag, from the end to the heading by bringing the striped corner of the folded edge to meet the open edge.

5. The outer point is turned inward parallel with the open edge, forming a second triangle.

6. Repeat the triangular folding until the entire length of the flag is folded.

7. When the flag is completely folded only the triangular blue field should be visible.

CARE OF YOUR FLAG

The life of your flag depends on your care. Dirt can cut fabrics, dull colors, and cause wear. Most outdoor flags can be washed in mild detergent and thoroughly rinsed. Indoor and parade flags should be dry-cleaned. Many dry cleaners offer free cleaning of U.S. flags during the months of June and July. Damaged flags can be repaired and utilized as long as the overall dimensions are not noticeably altered. American Legion posts and local governments often have facilities to dispose of unserviceable flags. Store your flags in a well-ventilated area away from any harsh chemicals or cleaning compounds. If your flag gets wet, never store it until it is completely dry. Wet folds cause permanent creases. Dampness ruins fabric and causes mildew. Pole care is also related to flag care. Rust and scale cause permanent stains, and some metallic oxides actually eat holes in fabric.

The life of your flag depends on your care.

SIZES OF FLAGS

The size of the flag is determined by the exposed height of the flagpole from which it is flying. The only consideration is for the flag to be in proper proportion to its pole. Flags which fly from angled poles on homes and those that are displayed on standing poles in offices and other indoor displays are usually either 3' x 5' or 4' x 6'. Color guards usually carry flags measuring 4' x 6'. Other recommended sizes are shown in the following table:

Flagpole Height (ft.) / Flag Size (ft.)

20 / 4 x 6	25 / 5 x 8
40 / 6 x 10	50 / 8 x 12
60 / 10 x 15	70 / 12 x 18
90 / 15 x 25	125 / 20 x 30
200 / 30 x 40	250 / 40 x 50

FLAG DAY

Each year on June 14, we celebrate the birthday of the Stars and Stripes, which came into being on June 14, 1777. At that *June 14 is* time, the Second Continental Congress *Flag Day.* authorized a new flag to symbolize the new nation, the United States of America.

The Stars and Stripes first flew in a Flag Day celebration in Hartford, Connecticut, in 1861, during the first summer of the Civil War. The first national observance of Flag Day occurred June 14, 1877, the centennial of the original flag resolution.

By the mid-1890s the observance of Flag Day on June 14 was a popular event. Mayors and governors began to issue proclamations in their jurisdictions to celebrate this event.

In the years to follow, public sentiment for a national Flag Day observance greatly intensified. Numerous patriotic societies and veterans groups became identified with the Flag Day movement. Since their main objective was to stimulate patriotism among the young, schools were the first to become involved in flag activities.

In 1916 President Woodrow Wilson issued a proclamation calling for a nationwide observance of Flag Day on June 14. It was not until 1949 that Congress made this day a permanent observance by resolving "that the 14th day of June of each year is hereby designated as Flag Day." The measure was signed into law by President Harry Truman.

Although Flag Day is not celebrated as a federal holiday, Americans everywhere continue to honor the history and heritage it represents.

AMERICAN FLAG TIMELINE

★ ★ ★ ★ ★ ★ ★ ★ ★ ★ ★ ★ ★

June 14, 1777

The Marine Committee of the Second Continental Congress passed its Flag Resolution, intended to establish a design of an ensign to be used on boats during the Revolutionary War:

> *"Resolved: that the flag of the United States be thirteen stripes, alternate red and white; that the union be thirteen stars, white in a blue field, representing a new constellation."*

The thirteen stars and thirteen stripes represented the thirteen original states: Delaware, Pennsylvania, New Jersey, Georgia, Connecticut, Massachusetts, Maryland, South Carolina, New Hampshire, Virginia, New York, North Carolina, and Rhode Island.

★ ★
1794

The Flag Act of 1794 (1 Stat. 341) was signed into law by President George Washington on January 13, 1794:

New States

Delaware
December 7, 1787
Pennsylvania
December 12, 1787
New Jersey
December 18, 1787
Georgia
January 2, 1788
Connecticut
January 9, 1788
Massachusetts
February 6, 1788
Maryland
April 28, 1788
South Carolina
May 23, 1788
New Hampshire
June 21, 1788
Virginia
June 25, 1788
New York
July 26, 1788
North Carolina
November 21, 1789
Rhode Island
May 29, 1790

Vermont
March 4, 1791
Kentucky
June 1, 1792

An Act Making an Alteration in the Flag of the United States

Be it enacted by the Senate and House of Representatives of the United States of America in Congress Assembled, That from and after the first day of May, Anno Domini, one thousand seven hundred and ninety-five, the flag of the United States, be fifteen stripes alternate red and white. That the Union be fifteen stars, white in a blue field.

The flag was changed to reflect the addition of Vermont and Kentucky. For a while, for aesthetic reasons, the number of stars and stripes was not changed when subsequent states joined the Union.

1814

The Star-Spangled Banner. The sight of the fifteen-star, fifteen-stripe flag on the morning of September 13, following the bombardment of Fort McHenry by British ships in Chesapeake Bay, inspired thirty-five-year-old Francis Scott Key to write a four-stanza poem, "Defence of Fort McHenry," which later became "The Star-Spangled Banner."

★ ★ ★ ★ ★

1818

The Flag Act of 1818 (3 Stat. 415) was

enacted by Congress on April 4, 1818. It provided for the rule that has remained to the present day of having thirteen stripes to represent the original thirteen colonies and having the number of stars match the number of states. It also provided that any change in the number of stars would be made on the following Independence Day.

An Act to establish the flag of the United States

Be it enacted by the Senate and House of Representatives of the United States of America, in Congress Assembled, That from and after the fourth day of July next, the flag of the United States be thirteen horizontal stripes, alternate red and white: that the union be twenty stars, white in a blue field.

And be it further enacted, That on the admission of every new state into the Union, one star be added to the union of the flag; and that such addition shall take effect of the fourth day of July then next succeeding such admission.

The new flag has twenty stars and thirteen stripes (the stripes remain at thirteen hereafter).

New States

Illinois
December 3, 1818

★
1819
21 stars

Alabama
December 14, 1819
Maine
March 15, 1820

★ ★
1820
23 stars

Missouri
August 10, 1821

★
1822
24 stars

Arkansas
June 15, 1836

★
1836
25 stars

Michigan
January 26, 1837

★
1837
26 stars

Florida
March 3, 1845

★
1845
27 stars

Texas
December 29, 1845

★
1846
28 stars

Iowa
December 28, 1846

★
1847
29 stars

New States

★
1848
30 stars

Wisconsin
May 29, 1848

★
1851
31 stars

California
September 9, 1850

★
1858
32 stars

Minnesota
May 11, 1858

★
1859
33 stars

Oregon
February 14, 1859

★
1861
34 stars

Kansas
January 29, 1861

★
1863
35 stars

West Virginia
June 20, 1863

★
1865
36 stars

Nevada
October 31, 1864

★
1867
37 stars

Nebraska
March 1, 1867

New States

Colorado
August 1, 1876

★
1877
38 stars

North Dakota
November 2, 1889
South Dakota
November 2, 1889

★ ★ ★ ★ ★
1890
43 stars

Montana
November 8, 1889
Washington
November 11, 1889

★
1891
44 stars

Idaho
July 3, 1890
Wyoming
July 10, 1890
Utah
January 4, 1896

★
1896
45 stars

Oklahoma
November 16, 1907

★
1908
46 stars

New Mexico
January 6, 1912
Arizona
February 14, 1912

★ ★
1912
48 stars

1931
"The Star-Spangled Banner" becomes
America's national anthem.

Alaska
January 3, 1959

★
1959
49 stars

Hawaii
August 21, 1959

★
1960
50 stars